FOREST
BOOKS
London 1990

Baudelaire's
PARIS

Verse translation by
Laurence Kitchin

Published by Forest Books
20 Forest View, Chingford, London E4 7AY, U.K.

First published 1990

Typeset by Cover to Cover, Cambridge
Printed by Dot Press Ltd, Oxford

Translations © Laurence Kitchin
Cover design © Dot Press Ltd, Oxford

British Library Cataloguing in Publication Data:
Baudelaire, Charles 1821–1867
Baudelaire's Paris: poems.
I. Title
841.8

ISBN 0 948259 97 3

Contents

To Brenda Walker

Introduction
Baudelaire: Poet of the City

Charles Baudelaire (1821–1867) was, among other things, the supreme poet of the inner city. His own was Paris. As he grew up, its architectural magnificence was under threat from overcrowding and pollution attendant on the age of steam. There had always been extremes of wealth and poverty in Paris. Now they grew worse, and what soon became an inspiration to Dickens across the Channel acquired a French accent. Poets, slow to perceive what was happening to their city, kept their distance, escaping outwards to nature and inwards to morbid psychology. Baudelaire, a mainstream Romantic, added realism, an unflinching gaze on what urban life had become.

In the first poem of this collection, ironically titled 'Landscape', and in the fifth, a part of 'Autumn Song', he occupies the foreground, stuck in Paris but a prey to contrasting moods: imagining escape into sunlight or dreading the onset of winter, foretold by the sound of firewood being chopped in the courtyard below his room. For 'Morning Twilight' and 'Evening Twilight', however, Baudelaire himself is withdrawn, and the effect is a Shakespearean blend of horror and compassion, which could apply to all inner cities, including the London of 1990 with its homeless lodged in cardboard boxes.

Of course cities also provide fleeting encounters of the kind Thomas Hardy noted when he remarked on the beauty of women glimpsed in the London tube never to be seen again. To the reader stunned by the impact of the 'Twilight' poems, Baudelaire's 'To a Passer-by' should come as welcome relief. Continuing this modulation into more intimately personal concerns, I have added three sonnets by

Symbolist poets, who illustrate the reverse of Baudelaire's objective realistic vein. Their reaction to the urban nightmare was retreat into the private self, into fine-spun, infinitely delicate lyrics. Gérard de Nerval (1808–1855) grappled with insanity, notably in 'The Dispossessed', where crossing the river Acheron symbolises recovery from two of his bouts of madness. Paul Verlaine (1844–1896) and a Spanish follower, Juan Ramón Jiménez (1881–1958) capture moods as elusive as butterflies.

Laurence Kitchin

Charles Baudelaire

Paysage

Je veux, pour composer chastement mes églogues,
Coucher auprès du ciel, comme les astrologues,
Et, voisin des clochers, écouter en rêvant
Leurs hymnes solennels emportés par le vent.
Les deux mains au menton, du haut de ma mansarde,
Je verrai l'atelier qui chante et qui bavarde;
Les tuyaux, les clochers, ces mâts de la cité,
Et les grands ciels qui font rever d'éternité.

Il est doux, à travers les brumes, de voir naître
L'étoile dans l'azur, la lampe a la fenêtre,
Les fleuves de charbon monter au firmament
Et la lune verser son pâle enchantement.
Je verrai les printemps, les étés, les automnes;
Et quant viendra l'hiver aux neiges monotones,
Je fermerai partout portières et volets
Pour bâtir dans la nuit mes féeriques palais.
Alors je rêverai des horizons bleuâtres,

Des jardins, des jets d'eau pleurant dans les albâtres,
Des baisers, des oiseaux chantant soir et matin,
Et tout ce que l'Idylle a de plus enfantin.
L'Emeute, tempêtant vainement a ma vitre,
Ne fera pas lever mon front de mon pupitre;
Car je serai plongé dans cette volupté
D'evoquer le Printemps avec ma volonté,
De tirer un soleil de mon coeur, et de faire
De mes pensers brulants une tiède atmosphère.

Landscape

I need, for eclogues meant to edify,
Like astrologers, a lodging near the sky.
I'll listen, close to belfries, in a daze
To solemn anthems which the wind relays.
High in my attic, hands upon my chin,
I'll see vibrations from the workshops' din,
Drainpipes and belltowers, mastheads of the town,
And the great sky where timeless visions drown.

It's good to see reborn through mist and damp
In the blue a star, in the window pane a lamp,
Rivers of smoke climbing the vaults of space
And magic poured out from the moon's pale face.
I'll see the spring, the summer and the fall;
When winter spreads the snow's unvaried pall,
I'll fasten every door and window tight
To build fantastic palaces all night.

Then I will dream horizons tinged with blue,
Gardens, and marble fountains weeping dew,
Kisses, and birdsong at sunrise and set,
Idyllic images more childish yet.
Rebellion, storming outside in its rage,
Won't even make me look up from my page.
Of these lone pleasures I will take my fill
To call up springtime by an act of will,
To tear a sun from my own heart and clear
By burning thought a temperate atmosphere.

Le Crépuscule du Matin

La diane chantait dans les cours des casernes,
Et le vent du matin soufflait sur les lanternes.
C'était l'heure ou l'essaim des rêves malfaisants
Tord sur leurs oreillers les bruns adolescents;
Où, comme un oeil sanglant qui palpite et qui bouge,
La lampe sur le jour fait une tache rouge;
Ou l'âme, sous le poids du corps revêche et lourd,
Imite les combats de la lampe et du jour.
Comme un visage en pleurs que les brises essuient,
L'air est plein du frisson des choses qui s'enfuient,
Et l'homme est las d'écrire et la femme d'aimer.

Les maisons cà et là commencaient a fumer.
Les femmes de plaisir, la paupière livide,
Bouche ouverte, dormaient de leur sommeil stupide;
Les pauvresses, traînant leurs seins maigres et froids,
Soufflaient sur leurs tisons et soufflaient sur leurs doigts.
C'était l'heure où parmi le froid et la lésine
S'aggravent les douleurs des femmes en gésine;
Comme un sanglot coupé par un sang écumeux
Le chant du coq au loin déchirait l'air brumeux;
Une mer de brouillards baignait les édifices,
Et les agonisants dans le fond des hospices
Poussaient leur dernier râle en hoquets inégaux.
Les débauchés rentraient, brisés par leurs travaux.
L'aurore grelottante en robe rose et verte
S'avançait lentement sur la Seine déserte,
Et le sombre Paris, en se frottant les yeux,
Empoignait ses outils, vieillard laborieux.

Morning Twilight

Reveillé sounded from each barrack square
And street lamps flickered in the morning air.
It was the time when writhing dreams in swarms
Pollute half-waking adolescent forms;
The reading lamp, a pulsing bloodshot eye,
Makes a red stain upon the whitening sky;
Then the soul, restless under body's weight,
Echoes the reading lamp's and dawn's debate.
Like a face drying after tears all night
The air is quivering with things in flight.
Man's had enough of writing, woman of bed.

Smoke went up here and there as homely fires were fed
Women of pleasure, dull and bleary eyed,
Slept in a stupor, gross lips gaping wide.
Poor, shrunken women bent rheumatic arms,
Blew on infusions, blew upon their palms.
It was the hour when cold and landlord's gain
Persecute women in pre-natal pain.
Far off, like sobs cut short by frothing blood,
A cock's crow ripped apart the misty flood.
The fog drenched all the buildings like a sea,
Moribund rejects of society
Hiccuped their last death rattles, out of sight.
Dissolute men reached home, disrupted in the night.

Shivering dawn, attired in rose and green
Moved slow across the Seine's deserted scene.
Dismal, laborious, blinking through the murk,
Old Paris grabbed his tools and set to work.

Le Crépuscule du Soir

Voici le soir charmant, ami du criminel;
Il vient comme un complice, à pas de loup; le ciel
Se ferme lentement comme une grande alcôve,
Et l'homme impatient se change en bête fauve.

O soir, aimable soir, désiré par celui
Dont les bras, sans mentir, peuvent dire: Aujourd'hui
Nous avons travaillé! – C'est le soir qui soulage
Les esprits que dévore une douleur sauvage,
Le savant obstiné dont le front s'alourdit,
Et l'ouvrier courbé qui regagne son lit.

Cependant des démons malsains dans l'atmosphère
S'éveillent lourdement, comme des gens d'affaire,
Et cognent en volant les volets et l'auvent.
A travers les lueurs que tourmente le vent
La Prostitution s'allume dans les rues;
Comme une fourmilière elle ouvre ses issues;

Partout elle se fraye un occulte chemin,
Ainsi que l'ennemi qui tente un coup de main;
Elle remue au sein de la cité de fange
Comme un ver qui dérobe a l'Homme ce qu'il mange.
On entend cà et là les cuisines siffler,
Les théâtres glapir, les orchestres ronfler;
Les tables d'hôte, dont le jeu fait les délices,
S'emplissent de catins et d'escrocs, leurs complices,
Et les voleurs, qui n'ont ni trêve ni merci,
Vont bientôt commencer leur travail, eux aussi,
Et forcer doucement les portes et les caisses
Pour vivre quelques jours et vêtir leurs maitresses.

Recueille-toi, mon âme, en ce grave moment,
Et ferme ton oreille a ce rugissement.
C'est l'heure ou les douleurs des malades s'aigrissent!
La sombre Nuit les prend à la gorge; ils finissent
Leur destinée et vont vers le gouffre commun;
L'hopital se remplit de leurs soupirs. – Plus d'un
Ne viendra plus chercher la soupe parfumée,
Au coin du feu, le soir, aupres d'une âme aimée.
Encore la plupart n'ont jamais connu
La douceur du foyer et n'ont jamais vécu!

Evening Twilight

Sweet evening's here, the criminal's ally,
Partner in crime, with vulpine gait; the sky
Slowly blots out as curtains hide the stage
And restless man assumes a bestial rage.

Evening long waited for when labourers can say,
Their very arms articulate: 'Today
We have worked hard!' – It's evening brings relief
To spirits eaten by a savage grief,
To the stubborn scholar's overweighted head
And the bent workman limping back to bed.

Meanwhile unhealthy demons in the murk
Like businessmen wake sluggishly to work
And bump against the shutters in their flight
Across the windblown streetlamp's fitful light.
Now Prostitution sets the streets ablaze;
Like an ant's nest it issues many ways;

It clears everywhere a hidden track,
Like an insurgent ready to attack;
It stirs the bosom of the filthy town
As a worm unveils to Man what he gulps down.
You hear a hissing as the kitchens heat,
The drone of orchestras, the theatres' bleat;
Round gamblers who dice away their goods
The tables fill with hookers and their hoods.
Robbers — no truce or mercy in that hell —
Will soon begin their labouring as well,
And delicately open tills and doors
To earn a few days' keep and dress their whores.

Compose yourself, my soul, at this grave time,
Be deaf to the primaeval howls of crime.
This is an hour of crisis for the ill!
Grim Night is at their windpipe; they fulfil
Their fate; all men's engulfment is begun;
The wards are dense with sighs; ah, more than one
Never again will seek the fragrant bowl
At evening by his hearth with a beloved soul.
That was for most of them a joy unknown:
Homeless, they never lived; and died alone!

À une Passante

La rue assourdissante autour de moi hurlait.
Longue, mince, en grand deuil, douleur majestueuse,
Une femme passa, d'une main fastueuse
Soulevant, balançant le feston et l'ourlet;

Agile et noble, avec sa jambe de statue.
Moi, je buvais, crispé comme un extravagant,
Dans son œil, livide, où germe l'ouragan,
La douleur qui fascine et le plaisir qui tue.

Un éclair . . . puis la nuit! — Fugitive beauté
Dont le regard m'a fait soudainement renaître,
Ne te verrai-je plus que dans l'éternité?

Ailleurs, bien loin d'ici! trop tard! *jamais* peut-être!
Car j'ignore où tu fuis, tu ne sais où je vais,
Ô toi que j'eusse aimée, ô toi qui le savais!

To a Passer-by

The deafening street assailed me with its yell.
Tall, slim, queenly in mourning, there glided past
A woman, deft and fastidious, holding fast
Her hem and trimmings as they rose and fell,

Agile and noble with her sculptured thigh.
I, shrivelled to a husk of raging thirst,
Drank from her eye, where hurricanes are nursed,
Grief that enthrals and pleasure's mortal sigh.

Lightning — and then the night! Beauty that strides away,
Whose glance has made me suddenly grow tall,
Shall I not see you till the judgment day?

Elsewhere, and far from here! Too late! Or *not at all!*
I don't know where you fled, nor you which way I go.
O you I could have loved, who knew that it was so!

Chant d'Automne

Bientôt nous plongerons dans les froides ténèbres;
Adieu, vive clarté de nos étés trop courts!
J'entends déjà tomber avec des chocs funèbres,
Le bois retentissant sur le pavé des cours.

Tout l'hiver va rentrer dans mon être: colère,
Haine, frissons, horreur, labeur dur et forcé,
Et, comme le soleil dans son enfer polaire,
Mon cœur ne sera plus qu'un bloc rouge et glacé.

J'écoute en frémissant chaque bûche qui tombe;
L'échafaud qu'on bâtit n'a pas d'écho plus sourd.
Mon esprit est pareil á la tour qui succombe
Sous les coups du bélier infatigable et lourd.

Il me semble, bercé par ce choc monotone,
Qu'on cloue en grande hâte un cercueil quelque part . . .
Pour qui? — C'était hier l'été; voice l'automne!
Ce bruit mystérieux sonne comme un départ.

Autumn Song

Soon we will plunge into the cold and dark.
Goodbye the living light of summer all too short!
Already I can hear the deadly crash of bark,
Of wood reverberating on the court.

Into my life winter returns entire:
Anger, hate, horror, labour in my cell,
And, like the sun trapped in its polar hell,
My heart will redden to a frozen fire.

I listen shivering to every log that falls;
A scaffold rises with no louder slam.
My spirit's like a tower's collapsing walls
Under the thud of the tireless battering ram.

Lulled by the monotone of shocking blows,
Someone hacks out a coffin, I believe.
For whom? Summer was yesterday; now autumn shows!
This eerie noise signals its time to leave.

Gérard
de Nerval

El Desdichado

Je suis le ténébreux, — le veuf, — l'inconsolé,
Le prince d'Aquitaine à la tour abolie:
Ma seule *étoile* est morte, — et mon luth constellé
Porte le *Soleil noir* de la *Mélancolie.*

Dans la nuit du tombeau, toi qui m'as consolé,
Rends-moi le Pausilippe et la mer d'Italie,
La *fleur* qui plaisait tant à mon cœur desolé,
Et la treille où le pampre à la rose s'allie.

Suis-je Amour ou Phebus? . . . Lusignan ou Biron?
Mon front est rouge encor du baiser de la reine;
J'ai rêvé dans la grotte où nage la sirène . . .

Et j'ai deux fois vainqueur traversé l'Acheron:
Modulant tour à tour sur la lyre d'Orphée
Les soupirs de la sainte et les cris de la fée.

The Dispossessed

I'm the bereaved, the shadow in despair,
The Prince of Aquitaine whose tower fell down;
This shining lute, my *star* no longer there,
Wears the *black sun* of *Melancholy's* frown.

You, my release from night and lethal air,
Give back Posillipo, the sea, the town,
The *flower* which comforted my sunless lair,
The trellis built for vine and rose to crown.

Am I Phoebus? Love? . . . Lusignan or Biron?
The queen's mouth still is red upon my brow,
Dreams from the sirens cave are with me now . . .

Twice as a conqueror I've crosses Acheron:
Stroking on Orpheus' lyre, now low, now high,
The saints deep sighing and the fairy's cry.

Paul
Verlaine

Colloque Sentimental

Dans le vieux parc solitaire et glacé,
Deux formes ont tout à l'heure passé.

Leurs yeux sont morts et leurs lèvres sont molles,
Et l'on entend à peine leurs paroles.

Dans le vieux parc solitaire et glacé,
Deux spectres ont évoqué le passé.

— Te souvient-il de notre extase ancienne?
— Pourquoi voulez-vous donc qu'il me'en souvienne?

— Ton cœur bat-il toujours à mon seul nom?
Toujours vois-tu mon âme en rêve? — Non.

— Ah! les beaux jours de bonheur indicible
Où nous joignions nos bouches! — C'est possible.

— Qu'il était bleu, le ciel, et grand l'espoir!
— L'espoir a fui, vaincu, vers le ciel noir.

Tels ils marchaient dans les avoines folles,
Et la nuit seule entendit leurs paroles.

Sentimental Conversation

In the old park, a solitude of snow,
Two forms passed by a moment ago.

Their lips are soft and their eyes are dead
You can scarcely overhear what is said.

In the old park, a solitude of snow,
Two spectres called back the long ago.

'Does this recall our passion of days gone by?'
'If you really want it to remind me, why?'

'Does my very name still make your heart beat so?
Even now do you see my soul when dreaming?' — 'No'.

'Ah, the fine days! Untold felicity
When our mouths joined themselves in one!' — 'Maybe'.

'How blue it was, the sky, the hope how vast!'
'Hope has fled, vanquished, to black overcast'.

So they walked onwards where the wild oats led,
And night, and only night, heard what they said.

Juan
Ramón
Jiménez

Retorno Fugaz

¿Cómo era, Dios mío, cómo era?
!Oh corazón falaz, mente indecisa! —
¿Era como el pasaje de la brisa?
Como la huida de la primavera?

Tan leve, tan voluble, tan lijera
cual estival vilano . . . Si! Imprecisa
con sonrisa que se pierde en risa . . .
!Vana en el aire, igual que una bandera!

Bandera, sonreir, vilano, alada
primavera de junio, brisa pura . . .
!Qué loco fué tu carnaval, que triste!

Todo tu cambiar trocóse en nada
—!memoria, ciega abeja de amargura!—
!No sé como eras, yo que sé que fuiste!

Fallacious Return

My God, what happened to us? Can I get it right?
— Oh lying heart and vacillating mind! —
Does it recall a breeze that passes by?
Or else the motion of the Spring in flight?

As weightless and as fickle and as slight
As summer thistledown . . . Yes! undefined
Like laughter as it leaves a smile behind . . .
Loose in the air, a banner gaining height!

A flag, a smile, thistledown on the wing,
Spring lost in June, a breeze's pure caress . . .
Oh, your mad carnival, in mourning draped!

All your transactions earn you not a thing
— Memory, that blind bee of bitterness! —
I, who can't add it up, know you escaped!